KINGFISHER DIPPERS

Submarines

David Jefferis

Kingfisher Books

Kingfisher Books, Grisewood and Dempsey Ltd,
Elsley House, 24–30 Great Titchfield Street,
London W1P 7AD.

First published in 1990 by Kingfisher Books

BRITISH LIBRARY CATALOGUING IN PUBLICATION DATA
Jefferis, David
   Submarines.
   1. Submarines
   I. Title II. Series
   623.8'257
ISBN 0-86272-508-9

Edited by Mike Halson
Designed by David Jefferis
Illustrated by Michael Roffe; Drawing Attention;
James Robins; Peter Stephenson/*Jillian Burgess*

Phototypeset by Southern Positives and Negatives (SPAN),
Lingfield, Surrey
Printed in Spain

Contents

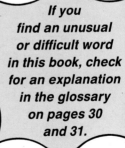

If you find an unusual or difficult word in this book, check for an explanation in the glossary on pages 30 and 31.

Dive, Dive, Dive!

You are in the cool and airy control room of a modern nuclear submarine, about to put to sea. In front of you, the Captain checks his computer screens for signs of any enemy submarines. Finding none, he gives the Officer of the Watch the order to dive. The hatches are shut, the periscopes lowered, and the tanks flooded with water. The deck begins to tilt down and the sub slips smoothly and quietly beneath the waves. You are off on your first submarine patrol!

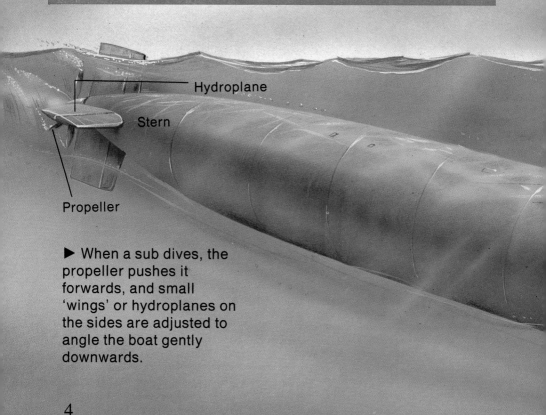

Hydroplane

Stern

Propeller

▶ When a sub dives, the propeller pushes it forwards, and small 'wings' or hydroplanes on the sides are adjusted to angle the boat gently downwards.

While underwater, a submarine is commanded from the control room in the heart of the boat. But when the sub is on the surface, it can also be commanded from the conning tower, inside the top part of the craft. From here, officers get a good view of the sea around them.

The upper section of a sub is known as the fin in the British Navy, but the sail in the US Navy.

▼ Two or more periscopes extend from the top of the fin. Using a periscope, an officer in the sub's control room can look out over the waves even though the sub is underwater.

Periscopes

Fin

▼ The front part of a submarine is called the bow. The rear is known as the stern. Fore is 'to the front' and aft is 'to the rear'. The floor is known as the 'deck'.

Hydroplanes

Bow

How a Submarine Works

A submarine goes up and down in the sea by using buoyancy tanks. To go under the surface, the tanks are flooded with water – the extra weight inside the craft allows the sub to sink.

   When it's time to come up again, water is blown out of the tanks by air carried on board. The air-filled tanks lighten the sub, so it rises to the surface. A dive-and-surface sequence is shown below.

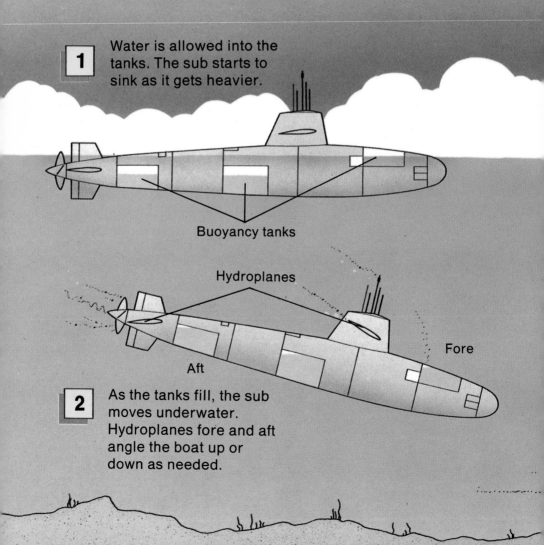

1 Water is allowed into the tanks. The sub starts to sink as it gets heavier.

Buoyancy tanks

Hydroplanes

Aft

Fore

2 As the tanks fill, the sub moves underwater. Hydroplanes fore and aft angle the boat up or down as needed.

BUOYANCY BALLOON

This experiment shows the lifting power of air in water. You will need the items shown on the right, as well as kitchen scales, a bucket of water – and an adult to give you some help.

Partly blow up the balloon and tie a knot in the neck. Make a 300-gram clay weight, and attach it with string 3cm below the balloon.

Put the balloon in the water. It should support the clay with ease. Keep adding more clay to see just how much the air will lift.

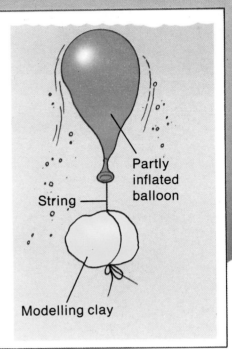

Partly inflated balloon

String

Modelling clay

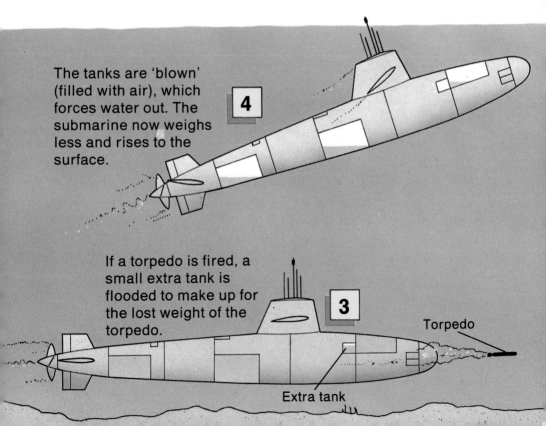

The tanks are 'blown' (filled with air), which forces water out. The submarine now weighs less and rises to the surface.

4

If a torpedo is fired, a small extra tank is flooded to make up for the lost weight of the torpedo.

3

Torpedo

Extra tank

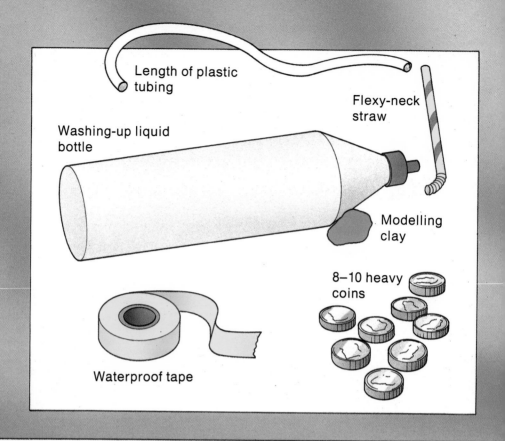

Length of plastic tubing

Flexy-neck straw

Washing-up liquid bottle

Modelling clay

8–10 heavy coins

Waterproof tape

The Dipper Diver

This model submarine, made with an empty washing-up liquid bottle, shows how buoyancy tanks work. Ask an adult to make several holes in the bottle in the positions shown. Then tape 4 or 5 heavy coins to either end. These will add weight to the craft and keep the holes facing the bottom. Fix a flexy-neck plastic straw to the bottle's nozzle, sealing it with modelling clay if necessary. To allow the sub to dive deep, add a length of plastic tube to the end of the straw. Stand by to flood tanks!

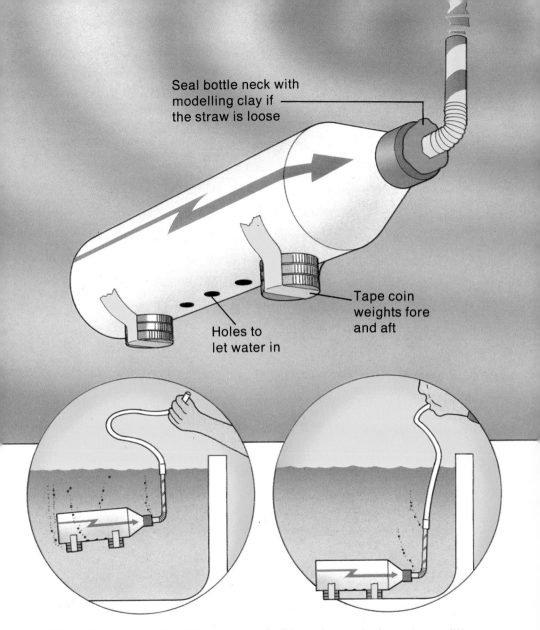

Seal bottle neck with modelling clay if the straw is loose

Tape coin weights fore and aft

Holes to let water in

▲ Once launched, the Dipper Diver will start to sink as water floods in through the holes along the bottom. Keep the end of the plastic tube above the waterline at all times.

▲ Blow through the tube to fill the Diver with air. It will start to rise as the water gets blown out. With practice, you will be able to make the Diver float at any depth you wish.

9

Early Submarines

Submarines came into general use in the early 1900s. Before then, there had been many experimental craft, including one made over 300 years ago by a Dutchman, Cornelius Drebbel. A rather nervous King James I of England travelled a short way down the River Thames in it, just below the surface.

The first use of a submarine in battle was in 1776, during the American War of Independence.

◀ David Bushnell's *Turtle* was used by the Americans to attack a British ship in New York Harbor in 1776. The idea was to sneak up underwater, screw a hook into the British ship's hull and attach a bomb. The attack failed as *Turtle's* screw couldn't get through the ship's metal plating. The sub was never used again.

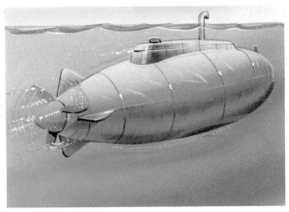

▲ The submarine built by Cornelius Drebbel in about 1620 was little more than a covered rowing boat, weighted so that it sloshed along only just underwater.

▲ The French *Gymnote*, launched in 1899, had electric motors. In 1906, the batteries blew up – the first (but not the last) such accident in submarine history.

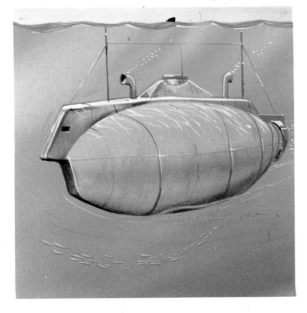

◄ *Holland Number 8* was launched in 1900. This American boat used petrol engines on the surface and electric motors under the water.

11

Subs at War

High-speed underwater weapons called torpedoes turned submarines into dangerous instruments of war. A sub commander could hunt for a ship, take aim using his attack periscope, then fire a torpedo to explode underwater against the target ship. In World War II, thousands of ships were sunk in this way. Modern torpedoes have computer controls in them to home in on a target, even if it is twisting and turning to escape.

▶ A World War II Sunderland aircraft attacks a German U-boat (named after the German word 'Unterseeboot', meaning undersea-boat). World War II subs mostly cruised on the surface, only diving for an attack or to escape battles like this one.

SUBMARINE NAVIGATION

When a sub has dived deep underwater, the periscopes are no longer of any use. In the past, navigators worked out their course using maps, often returning to the surface to check their position by the Sun or stars, or by compass.

Modern nuclear subs can navigate for weeks on end without surfacing. They use advanced computerized instruments which tell the navigation crew exactly where they are all the time.

The sub's officers also need to know what there is in the surrounding area. For this they rely on sensitive listening equipment called sonar.

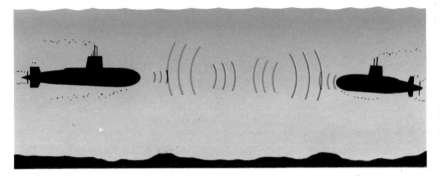

▲ Sonar works by sending out pings of sound into the water, and recording the size, shape and position of any objects which bounce the noise back as echoes. These may be rises and dips on the sea bed, schools of fish, whales – or another seagoing vessel.

► A sub's sonar pings risk being picked up by an enemy. Modern microphone equipment can listen out for engine noises without making any sound at all.

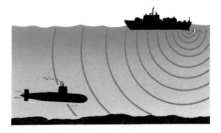

The Modern Submarine

Today's submarines are in service with the navies of many countries. The biggest as well as the fastest subs come from the USSR – Typhoons are underwater giants, as large as some ocean liners, while the smaller Alphas can speed along underwater at nearly 80 km/h. Most subs can manage at least 50 km/h.

Modern subs have two shells or hulls – the outer one in contact with the water, and a much thicker inner one for added protection.

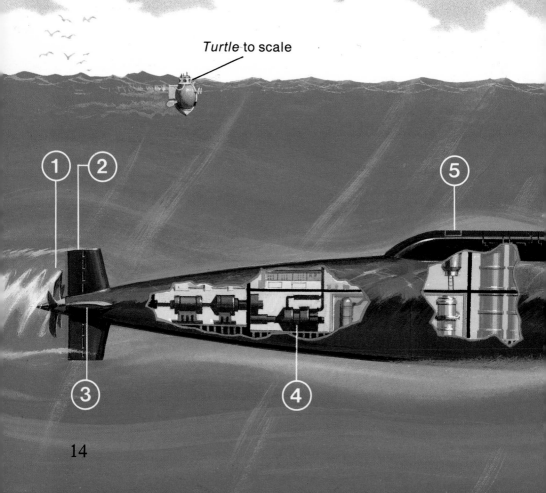

Turtle to scale

1. Propeller – pushes the sub through the water.
2. Rudder – steers the sub.
3. Hydroplanes – control the sub's angle in the water.
4. Engine room – power can be provided by a nuclear reactor, diesel engines or electric motors.
5. Emergency escape hatch.
6. Missile being test-fired – not all subs carry this kind of weapon.
7. Periscopes – search 'scopes give a long-range view, while attack 'scopes are for closer work.
8. Fin – contains the conning tower, periscopes and other equipment.
9. Living sections – include cooking, eating, exercise and sleeping areas.
10. Inner hull.
11. Outer hull.
12. Control room.
13. Navigation section.
14. Torpedo room.

On Patrol

Submarines which carry missiles often spend ten or more weeks at sea on one patrol. The Captain doesn't know where he is to go until he leaves port – and then he opens a sealed envelope which contains his secret instructions.

During a patrol, the crew are kept busy running the submarine, checking equipment and doing battle exercises. Life aboard is cramped, but the extra money paid to submariners helps to make up for the uncomfortable conditions.

▲ In the control room, officers control the boat and keep a check on what is going on. The boat is steered by helmsmen using rudder and hydroplane controls. Here, the Officer of the Watch looks out at the surface through a periscope.

▲ The engine room is to the rear of the sub, near the propeller. Like everywhere else in a sub, there is little spare space. The crew have to walk along narrow gangways.

► The galley is where all the crew's food is prepared. Fresh water is supplied by machines which take out the salt from seawater.

► The sleeping quarters are cramped, even on the biggest subs. The officers have their own cabins, while the sailors sleep in narrow bunks like those shown here.
   The crew keep themselves fit by using training equipment in a small gym.

Deepsea Explorers

Not all underwater craft are for naval use. Many are used by scientists or businesses and are called submersibles. Submersibles are often very small, with room for only two people. Others are bigger and may even make a temporary home for people working on the sea bed.

Scientific submersibles are used to increase our understanding of the seas and oceans. One of the most fascinating expeditions took place in 1960, when two scientists descended almost 11 kilometres beneath the waves in the submersible *Trieste*.

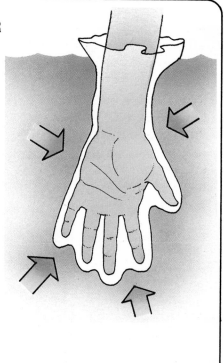

THE PRESSURE OF WATER

The weight of water at depth presses on a sub's steel hull with great force. Several craft have been lost when their hulls simply crumpled during deep dives.

This experiment lets you 'feel' water pressure.

First, find a smallish plastic bag and make sure it has no holes in it. Put one hand in the bag, then gently 'dive' your hand into a sink or bucket of cold water. You will feel the odd sensation of water squashing the bag tight against your hand.

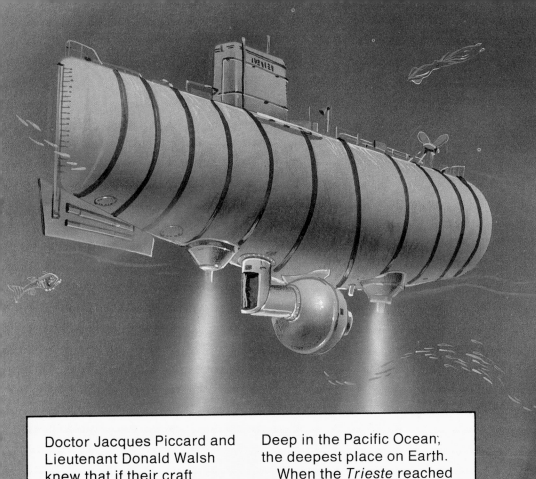

Doctor Jacques Piccard and Lieutenant Donald Walsh knew that if their craft leaked, they would be squashed flat as pancakes by the tremendous water pressure. It took them nearly five hours to descend to the bottom of the Challenger Deep in the Pacific Ocean, the deepest place on Earth.

When the *Trieste* reached the ocean floor, one of the scientists' main questions was answered almost straight away – a passing fish proved that life can exist even at that incredible depth.

19

Finding the *Titanic*

On the night of 14th April 1912, the passenger liner
Titanic collided with an iceberg. The jagged ice
ripped open the ship's hull and she sank into the
North Atlantic with the loss of over 1500 lives. The
wreck was not found until the summer of 1985 when
scientists, diving in the submersible *Alvin*,
discovered the shattered wreck. The sub had a robot
'floating eye' called *Jason Junior* to help in the
search. *Jason Junior* carried video cameras and
powerful floodlights to illuminate the scene.

As *Alvin* floats nearby, *Jason Junior* closes in to take close-up video pictures of the ghostly wreck. The robot eye is joined to *Alvin* by a cable, but has its own electric motors and propellers. Its actions are controlled by a scientist aboard *Alvin* sending signals down the control cable.

Sunlight only penetrates the upper layers of the oceans. It gets darker and colder as you dive deeper. At the bottom, the temperature is a steady 2.5°C.

Sunlit zone
Most sea creatures live near the surface.

Twilight zone
No seaweeds or other underwater plants grow below here.

Sunless zone
Utterly dark, except for a few glowing deep sea creatures. Some of these have luminous or shining lights on their bodies. These are used to attract other animals so they can be caught and eaten.

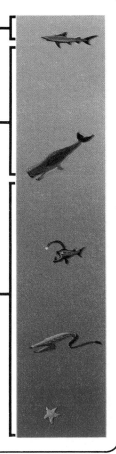

Rescue on the Sea Bed

Very occasionally, a submarine patrol ends in disaster. In 1963 the US sub *Thresher* went straight to the sea bottom after diving trials went wrong. At 2000 metres down, the water pressure was too great for any rescue to be possible and all the crew died.

Since then, several Deep Submergence Rescue Vehicles, or DSRVs, have been built for submarine emergencies. DSRVs cannot go as deep as the *Thresher* did, but they are still useful machines. A DSRV can lock onto a sub's emergency escape hatch and rescue 24 people at a time, from a maximum depth of 1500 metres.

▲ Submarine *XR-5* has sprung a leak and the crew cannot control her. Slowly the doomed boat settles on the ocean floor. At 1490 metres deep, the sub can just be reached by a DSRV.

A radio float is sent to the surface where it will send out an emergency signal. Now all the crew can do is hope the signal will soon be picked up by someone up above.

◀ The emergency signal is received by a navy ship and a big rescue operation swings into action. A DSRV is put aboard a military cargo plane, to be airlifted as near as possible to the stricken *XR-5*.

▼ The DSRV is loaded onto the back of a 'mother-sub', which will carry it below the surface.

▶ The 15 metre long DSRV slowly nears the *XR-5*. At last the helmsman locks his craft onto the escape hatch in front of *XR-5*'s fin. In a few moments, 24 of *XR-5*'s crew climb into the DSRV. The hatches are shut and the DSRV returns to its mother sub. Several trips will have to be made, but in a few hours the entire crew will have been saved.

Future Subs

Over the years, submarines have become bigger and bigger. Future designs are likely to be smaller, making them cheaper, faster and harder to detect.

Robot equipment will be used more and more. Unmanned machines are often a lot cheaper than those built for carrying people. Also, using robot equipment means that human beings are not exposed to the dangers of underwater work.

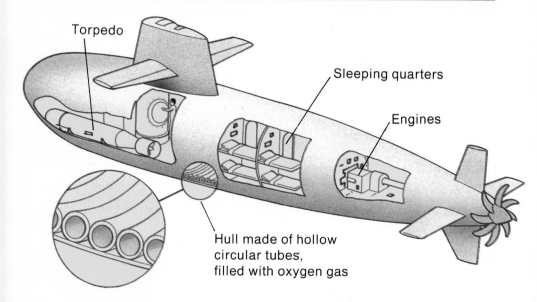

Torpedo

Sleeping quarters

Engines

Hull made of hollow circular tubes, filled with oxygen gas

▲ The GST is a mini-sub design. The craft stores oxygen gas, necessary for its diesel engines, in hollow tubes which also form its hull. The hollow tubes make the hull about five times stronger than normal, allowing the GST to dive deeply and safely. Waste gas from the engine can be stored in the hull tubes too, so it is not released into the water.

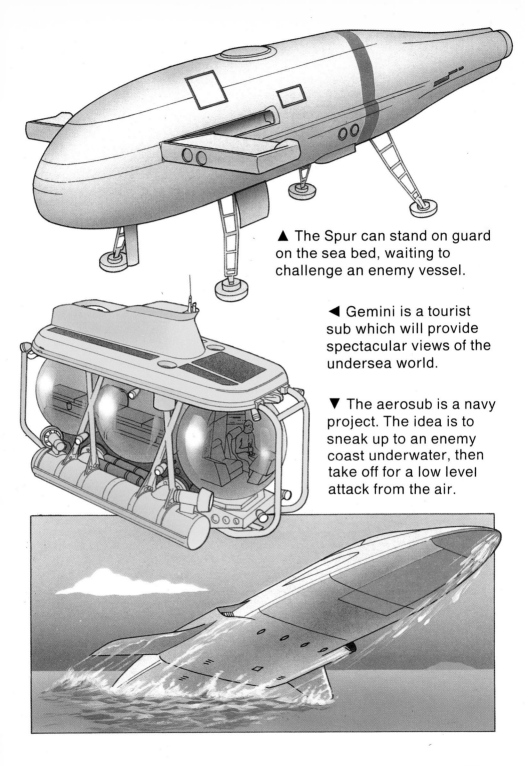

▲ The Spur can stand on guard on the sea bed, waiting to challenge an enemy vessel.

◀ Gemini is a tourist sub which will provide spectacular views of the undersea world.

▼ The aerosub is a navy project. The idea is to sneak up to an enemy coast underwater, then take off for a low level attack from the air.

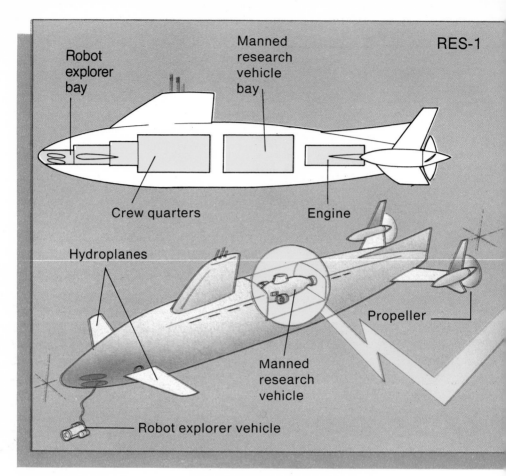

Robot explorer bay

Manned research vehicle bay

Crew quarters

Engine

Hydroplanes

Propeller

Manned research vehicle

Robot explorer vehicle

Design a Submarine

This is a possible design for the RES-1, a Research and Exploration Surveyor of the future. Try designing your own sub, using the RES-1 as a starting point. It has a smooth shape and two propellers for high-speed underwater cruising. It carries small robot explorer vehicles which can be sent out from bays in the bow section. Behind the fin, cargo doors unfold to reveal a manned research vehicle.

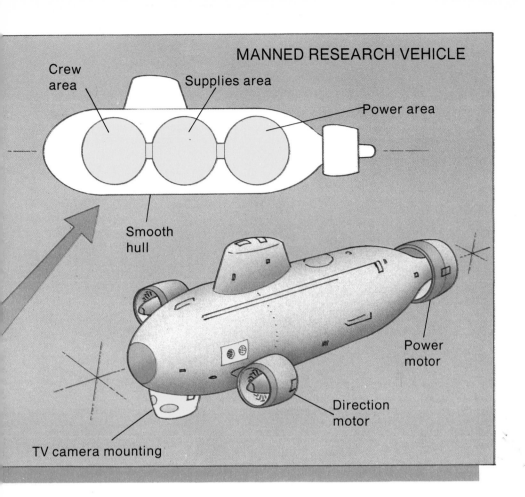

MANNED RESEARCH VEHICLE

Crew area

Supplies area

Power area

Smooth hull

Power motor

Direction motor

TV camera mounting

You can design your sub to work at high or slow speeds, but remember that fast subs should have smooth, gently rounded shapes to let them slip through the water like fish. For very slow speed work, subs can be any shape – real ones often look more like collections of spare parts than proper craft.

Subs Big and Small

Submarines have grown steadily in size from tiny one-man craft to the giant Russian Typhoon-class boats. The subs on this page show how sizes and styles have changed in the last 80 years or so.

◄ S-class, built 1910–1914. Used by the British, American and Polish navies.

► Type IXB U-boat. Built 1938–1944. Used by the German Navy during World War II.

► I-400 cruiser submarine. Used by Japan in World War II. Carried three seaplanes.

▼ George Washington-class, used by the US Navy. Five of these boats were launched in 1959 and 1960.

▼ Typhoon-class missile boat. At 170m long, the Typhoon is the world's biggest sub. Used by the Russian Navy.

◄ Future craft may well include tiny mini-subs such as the GST (shown in detail on page 24).

0 ⌞_____⌟ 20m
Scale

OTHER UNDERSEA MACHINES

Submersibles like these are used for all sorts of underwater jobs including exploration, surveying wrecks, laying pipelines, servicing oil rigs and repairing telephone cables.

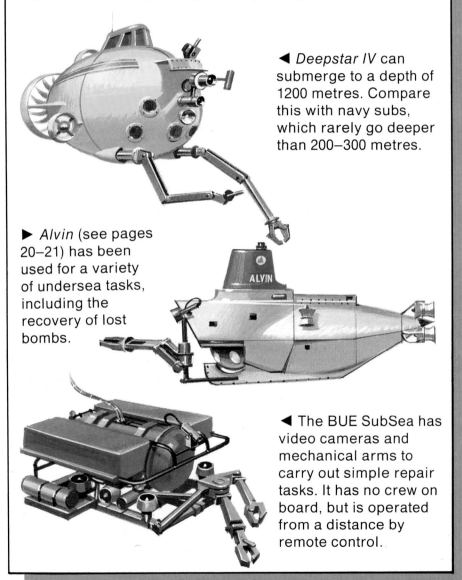

◀ *Deepstar IV* can submerge to a depth of 1200 metres. Compare this with navy subs, which rarely go deeper than 200–300 metres.

▶ *Alvin* (see pages 20–21) has been used for a variety of undersea tasks, including the recovery of lost bombs.

◀ The BUE SubSea has video cameras and mechanical arms to carry out simple repair tasks. It has no crew on board, but is operated from a distance by remote control.

Glossary

Bow
The front of a ship or sub. Pronounced like 'WOW'.

Buoyancy tanks
Internal tanks containing water or air. When flooded with water, the sub will dive. To rise, the water is 'blown' out with air. The sub's depth below the surface depends on the amount of water which is in the tanks.

Conning tower
A control area inside the fin. Used to command the vessel when the sub is travelling on the surface.

Diesel engines
Oil-fuelled engines much like those of a large truck. They are normally used to drive a sub when it is on the surface, as diesels need air and give off poisonous exhaust fumes. Diesels can be used at 'periscope depth' with a snorkel. This is a tube which sticks out of the water, letting air in and exhaust gases out. Diesels are also used for recharging submarine batteries, which power the electric motors needed for underwater work.

Exercises
Practice by armed forces. Subs often link with surface ships and aircraft in 'hide-and-seek' exercises, to test crews and equipment in case of real battle.

Fin
A tower-like section rising from the middle of a submarine. Contains the conning tower, periscopes and communication equipment. Also known as the sail.

Galley
Ship or submarine's kitchen. Crew eat in a restaurant area called the mess.

Helmsman
The person who steers a ship or a submarine. In a sub, one helmsman controls the rudder and another controls the hydroplanes.

Hull
The skin of a submarine. Modern subs have two hulls for extra strength and safety.

Hydroplanes
Mini 'wings' which control the angle of a submarine. They can also tilt a sub sideways, so when turning underwater it can bank into the turn like an aircraft.

Missile
A long-range rocket carried by many bigger submarines. Missiles can be fired while the sub remains submerged.

Nuclear reactor
Many modern subs run on nuclear energy. Inside a reactor, heat is generated from a small amount of 'radioactive' fuel. The heat is used to make electricity to supply all the power on board, from cooking and lighting to the electric motors in the engine room. Nuclear reactors are heavily shielded with concrete and metal to prevent invisible but highly dangerous rays leaking into the rest of the sub and harming the crew.

Periscope
A viewing device used in subs which pokes up above the waves to see what's happening on the surface. 'Periscope depth' is the maximum height of the periscope tube – around three metres. Below this, periscopes are lowered and the sub runs blind, relying on electronic equipment and charts of the sea bed.

Sonar
An echo-sounding system used to detect objects both underwater and on the surface.

Stern
The rear of a ship or sub.

Torpedo
A cylinder-shaped weapon with its own power and steering systems. Explodes on contact or when near its target. It is fired out of tubes in the forward section of a submarine, and only travels underwater.

U-boat
The word commonly used for a German submarine.

Index